4 BROWN GIRLS WHO WRITE

Sheena

Hope you enjoy!

Thank you! Love Roshni x

Sharan xx

Second Edition
Copyright © 2019 by FEM Press

Copyright © Roshni Goyate 2019
Copyright © Sharan Hunjan 2019
Copyright © Sunnah Khan 2019
Copyright © Sheena Patel 2019

Roshni Goyate, Sharan Hunjan, Sunnah Khan, Sheena Patel have asserted their rights to be identified as the authors of this Work in accordance with the Copyright, Designs and Patents Act 1988

This edition published in 2019
First published by FEM Press in 2018

ISBN: 978-1-91601-98-0-5

4 BROWN GIRLS WHO WRITE

**ROSHNI GOYATE
SHARAN HUNJAN
SUNNAH KHAN
SHEENA PATEL**

SILK	9
SAFFRON	27
SMOKE	47
TEMPLES	77

SILK

One day I'd like to be softer in my own skin

Run a bath and help myself in.
Run my fingers through my hair.
Apply oil to the roots.

Use the pressure of my Nana's palms.
A rough and shaking kind of love.
The kind of love that gives me whiplash
and tingles to the scalp.
The kind of love that isn't afraid to rub itself raw.

I'd like to throw the hard brush out.
Buy a silky sponge.
Lather between my legs and laugh
at my own jokes.

I'd dry between each of my toes.
Even the last one that looks like a growth.
I'd like to hold that one the most.

Sunnah

In winter I became white

but as soon as the sun
hit my skin

I felt the multiplication
of my melanin.

I felt it multiply
and fortify.

Sleeping under the sun
soaking gold

I wanted to eat it,
swallow heat and shine.

Then you asked me why
I didn't want to be mistaken

for being white:
it was a complicated answer.

White is right
there hiding under umbrellas

slapping on fifty plus to hide
white lies and dark truths

my aunties shouting
'Kali horkey aagi!'
(*You've come back black!*)

My entrenched fear of not being fair,
realising the colonising

complimented for being Fair&Lovely™
but how *unfair*, how *unlovely!*

Winter had occupied my city
snow coloured every street,

every tree, every dream,
until I looked down at my skin

noticing the sun
flowering up my melanin.

Sharan

A Song for Brown Alice

Brown Alice, when I wake
some days I swear I hear
you speaking sticky sweet tongues like
you're singing through molasses.
Blessed with agelessness we,
twinned in our separate ways,
grow together gently, ferociously
through the ages, and here in this age,
where everything is fraught, we
ought to be in the same time zone,
really babe
we ought to be
in the same
time zone.

Brown Alice, brown goddess, say
a prayer for me as I say one, two,
or a few for you, as I celebrate
you and wish you were this side
of midnight to become my personal
stylist. Give me strength.
Give me purpose.
Give me your sartorial blessings
and swagger for days, dear Alice.
Give me strength.

As I channel you under strobes
put firecrackers under my toes
and strings tug at my elbows
a playfulness unknown even
when in plain sight, I am
channeling you under strobes;
do you see me, mama?
Do you hear your very own
voice echoing between my
cheeks, do you feel me, mama?
Can you see me, writing this
song for you, will you see me
one day soon so I can sing it
directly to you.

Will you see me, mama?

Musky

your nose
on my sun seared skin
breathing me in
you say I smell
like no other
lips pursed tight
on my shoulder
every taste bud
on the tip
of your tongue
sticks to mine
sucker slow
as we kiss

Crotch Dreams

I like being near the brown
of your skin, I like the way the hair curls
around your crotch, fingers pointing this way and that.
Don't know which way to go down
the length of your legs to the bone where
the skin cracks likes a dry well and reminds me
of the village my mother was born in.
Or up through the undergrowth of under things sweating
before the sun touches it.

Strong hair.

Stronger than the hair on your chin you tell me and
I want to tell you that I don't carry
my shame on my face.
It's buried in the follicles between my legs. It takes
industrial strength wax and the pain
of all the ways I wish I was different
and even that feels like a punishment, even that
feels like a god damn sin.

What a sin is sin.

You brush the fur up on my neck, willing it to rise.
Willing it to catch the wind, to catch
the dust and the pollen and the wetness

of living things. To catch
the things that smooth skin can't.

You're hair is sticky even when you pull it out.

It oozes a truth I don't want to hear.
It oozes Persian poems written
in the backroom with the front door shut.

*Your smooth skin. It is your mouth
without its tongue.*

Baby Teeth

"Dandha!"
    It flew from my mouth
        like spit.
A tooth
    once lodged
        dug out
Baby teeth
    the shape of my mother's words
        my father's hard consonants.
They fell out
    one
        by
            one
stolen from under my pillow.

Like silver, my dreams were hard and cold.

Adult teeth grew
large wide overbearing
ugly braced tightened
new shapes new sounds
white white white.

Now it falls from my lips
drips from my tongue
steps out in dainty tiptoes

from the crowns
of my mouth.

When I smile at the world,
grinning blindly,
tooth to tooth

I don't recognise myself.

Fashionable

Your season is in season
the people love your spice.
Harissa, cumin, sriracha,
eye-watering pepper, oh, how nice.

Your flavour is in flavour
drawing crowds to festival shacks
to vans and huts and carts
selling your food behind your back.

What's trendy? Tell me, what's the new fad?
Your hues are being scrutinised
by thieves trying on your clothes,
thieves immune to being criticised.

Rules broken over centuries
like a bridge worn down by footsteps.
They have countless ways to fix you,
to save you and yours from yourselves.

While you heal and scar with love,
and you heal yourself again
they regress and poison with ego
and still the world revolves around them.

Roshni

And still the world turns, oblivious.
And still seasons change.
And still we're striving to mend.
And still we're a passing trend.

Being Brown is Back in Fashion

Sorry drop the *back*, come sit
at the front. Unfold your arms and grow
out your eyebrows.
We're in *season!*
Pakistani mangoes make your mouth sticky
with the taste of the sun.

We've been waiting all our lives
 with our hands on our waists
and our hips in the air.
That jingle isn't the bell,
we've been calling you
down the mountain for years
with the bracelets round our ankles.

Those goats, they're long dead
but we keep dancing
in those Swiss fields.
Cold toes, blue sky,
pink duputta flying high,
signaling south.

Shami Kapoor forever warming our hearts.

Sunnah

Mondello

You tasted of salt
I licked your neck,

like ice cream,
you melted.

We lay like thieves
taking the sun

your skin cracked, burned,
reddened, mine

deepened, flourished,
breathed...

Back home now, it's a secret
folded under my skin.

I carry it, or I wonder,
if it carries me.

An informal ode / in english /
to the two faces of your mouth

Part I

In your mouth
I find
lush green valleys
and heady mountain tops
where perilous cliff ledges
meet soft snowy drifts

I find
deep cool
rock pools
filled with creeping starfish
and feel the violent ocean surf
tangle the octopus

I find
whistling caves
of swirling bats
where amongst
the beat
of leathery wings
we paint
ochre
on the walls

Part II

I ate the pomegranate seeds
and I sank underground
to be with you

I see now
you hoard
the hearts
of others
taking them
with you
into this dark,
careful to
promise nothing

I see the bones
of my predecessors
hung
over doors
shamefully
decorating the walls
pitifully
pulsing with life

Mouthful
by
mouthful

you suck
out of the air
all the words
I ever said
to sustain
only you

You are
a coward

At your feet
I spit the
bitter seeds
I've rolled
gently
around
my tongue

I want the light
and the
brave sun
on my face

and my skeleton
in my body,
whole.

SAFFRON

Net Curtains

I hang these words out to dry
as you hung the net curtains
on the washing line
bleached from the sun.

In your salwaar kameez you kicked
the *caapu* along, it scraped
the paved garden ground
as you pegged the net neatly.

Words wash themselves, bathe in
holy water, drink, scrub themselves
clean. I hang them on this line
of washing to dry in the blazing heat

of breath, mine, theirs, yours.
Like your curtains they've become white.
They frame my stanza, a mesh, a net
washed white by our brown hands.

Thresholds

Two sets of mirrored eyes
ablaze in barely suppressed rage,
the brightly coloured plastic water gun
drip
drips at my side
the shrieks of play reverberate outside
of the walls of the house.
The neighbourhood boys and my brother
racing and pounding the streets
in a water gun fight.

But inside
the toy in my hand
drip drips
at my side
my eyes ablaze in rage.

You cannot play outside, you say
our legs astride meet length for length,
two cowboys across the plain
fingers tickle the air
the pant of my breath fills the room;
my eyes narrow,
lips curl,
teeth are bared
my nostrils twitch like the lid on a boiling pot,

whistle whistle whistle
tickle tickle tickle.

I will smash you to smithereens
you maternal blockade,
smash you
I cry in my head.

Why.
Not.
The words escape
from the gaps in my teeth.

I don't want you to play
with the neighbour's kids,
you say.

Something breaks in you
and breaks in me
I see your eyes
slip down a ledge
into vulnerability.

I was touched by the neighbour
you softly say,
when I was your age.

The silence beats a metal shape

I can't see.
Your body slackens in pain
mine hardens
fighting the nausea
that rears its head.

I say nothing
and walk out of the room to play
with the neighbourhood kids instead.

We Were Made By What We Were Not

We weren't godless and we weren't *gorae*
We weren't parties or pinafores and we definitely weren't
Christmas
We weren't Indian movies or Eastenders
We weren't haggis and we certainly were not whisky
We weren't like the neighbours and we weren't like our friends
We weren't cats or dogs *Chi chi gundi billy*
Wash your hands, you're not like them
Go do your homework

We were get in the back room
Set the table
Have you done your namaz?
Sometimes we were Anne of Green Gables
And that one winter we were schools closed
Socks on hands
Sledging down Grampian way in bin bags

We were *gutter gutter hai hai*
Nana's hands cracked in flour
Fetch the tuva
We were white and brown
Soft and round
Chapattis

But regardless of what they told us we were
Or we were not - I remember you

You were football and I was stories
You were laugh out loud, I was write it down
You were leave me alone I was hug me I'm hurting
We were day dreams and rebellious schemes
We were sneak out the back door, make for a dance floor

We were the worlds out there
Noses pressed against glass

A Steal

Dad tells me all he wants,
all he's saved for all his life,
is to give his children

all his children

their own good, big wedding.

He tells me this
as we drive home in my new Honda Jazz.
I saved up to buy it.
Found it on Auto Trader, a steal,
five minutes from home.

He drives it to the driveway in Wembley

to the home where he married my mother,
Penniless. Family-less. All I can think is
I wish I could afford a house
on the same street. Or a PhD.

Demeter,
Your Daughter Wanted to Go.

And the beat
of your galloping maternal heart
whisked away by darkness,
by force; or, worse yet,
disappeared by choice.

The rhythmic drum
deep within your chest
falls silent now
as you sit on the crooked boughs
of this willow tree.

Unable to weep
you sob and choke
your back broken by grief, by love
and now
by its absence.

The leaves whistle in the wind
carrying your wails through the seasons
into time unformed,
you thrust your sharded heart
into the ground,
your hands are
cut and bleeding.

Sheena

Never again
will the crops grow,
the flower heads will not shine their faces into the sun.
Never again will bread be broken
the corn heads will stunt
the earth cracked and forsaken.
Never again will a light smile
play upon your face
with your beloved removed
below the ground
Never again.
Never again.
Never again.

How Now Brown Cow

Early on, I came to understand.
That to align myself with English words
was to walk out free, no curfew or curry smells
chasing me down the street.

English was my bestest subject.

I'd write stories and poems.
Stuff them in my bag, press them earnestly
into the palms of tired teachers.
Recite them on my solitary walks, to the birds
who pulled worms and listened with darting attention.

You told me
it was because there were some words
I just wouldn't understand.
That I couldn't *possibly* understand.
You told *them*
that even though I was good at pretending
there was something *missing*.

English, is not her first language.

Which one came first?
I couldn't remember.
I remember my grandfather slapping my back,

making guttural sounds as he bounced
me on his knee and I remember the way my mother's voice sang
rainbow songs as she threw me up to touch the sky
and my forehead resting on a prayer mat somewhere.
Letting the melody of that other world reverberate
in the nostrils of the Imam and bounce
around my chest.

What were the first sounds to reach my ears?
What were the first words I learnt to curl
around my tongue, that slipped from my dribbling mouth?

I imagined the beat of my mothers heart, belly full
of turqa dhal and Tunnocks tea cakes. Blood full
of duty and quiet rebellion, of heartache
and muttered prayers, of hope. So much hope.

In what language did you sing to your swollen belly?
What colour were your tears? Did you dream me up
in Punjabi or English? Did you seal a kiss
on my father's lips with a Persian prayer?

What language was I born of?

From Father, Forever Changed
(For Lizzie)

Here is a parcel gifted with thought
it pours silver smoke machine-style
sheer enough to enter through skin
and nestle like a pregnant wild cat
ready to give birth to a litter of
sonic kittens. They grow and
gently prowl, softly roll in playfight
making paw-print, fur-print
impressions on my mind. This is

Horses. This is life-changing this
is crippling awe, unable to move
no matter how many times I
listen because every time is
different, every time there's a new
note, every time there's an unheard
soundling changing the landscape
urging me to look upon her voice
once more and look again and look
again and fall in love all over again
with crippling awe, crippling other
than arms up in the air, drinking
it through fingertips, drowning in
well-worn lyrics, melodies that
shaped my vocal chords and

balanced chemicals in brain. This is
Patti. She is from
father. I am
forever changed.

Chaudavin Ka Chand
(The Moon of the Fourteenth Lunar Night)

I.

I brushed your hair under the blue moon.
Pulled out tired curls said
Mama it will be okay, I promise.

I tried to fall asleep in that room with no windows
but the light of the old gas heater buzzing red,
made long shadows of my fears.

I pulled the covers over my head,
pressed my face against the cold cotton
of your kameez, pushed up against your chest
and listened to cat fights in the night
and your heart beat announcing.

II.

Beyond. The men are on their knees.
Whispering prayers into the dirt.
Rocking back and forth
they make waves of their grief
filling their mouths
with old words and sweet chai.

Tears blur my view
but I know you are there, alone, in white.
Some strange vision in the moonlight.

Frogs burp. The men pray on.
Women whimper
and you lie there.
As if it was some small thing.
As if this blood was not your blood.

You lie there, with your rubber skin and your old bones
and holy threads where your eyes should be.

The moon is full.
My mouth is empty.
Your eyes are closed. I pinch my own skin and wonder
what you were waiting for.

Before I kissed you this morning.
Before they washed you like it was the first time.
Before I told you it would be okay.

Old Home Sonnet

Two owls sit on a branch on your card.
Pink sky, glasses perch on the nose of one,
the wiser, wordier, worthier. Hearts
float in the air. When we visit the home
someone throws up white, others pray for their souls.
You lie, legs like sticks, scrunched under covers,
face clean and bright with skin brown and gold
while a fat sickly smell sits in old corners.

I stare at fumbling   mumbling   hands   words well
up jumbled stumbled   eyes crumbled legs   crumpled
time outnumbered   faces   remembered
memories   dismembered
                       like the hip that broke
                                when you fell.

Sharan

If Amitabh Bachan was My Father

If Amitabh Bachan was my father
He wouldn't have just called me after six months
Only to hang up on me
He would have made a much bigger deal out of it

If Amitabh Bachan was my father
I'd call him Abu and he'd call me Rani
We'd have written a song about our long distance relationship
And danced out the things that we didn't have the words for

Smoking a Cheeky Fag in My Parents' Garden
on a Cool September Midnight After a Breakup

The hum where the Harrow Road meets the
North Circ whispers secrets of transition tonight
until the clumsy, clattered rattle
of the Bakerloo chimes in marking
the aliveness of London's midnight.
To the left, a sliver of the Stadium
greets me through trees with steely hello.
To the right, the waning moon
forces its way through broken cloud.
Waning like the potted plants of Dad's
summer glory. Like the almost warmth of July now
tickling my fingertips with gentle icy kiss.
This is my homeland. This is my abode.
This cigarette is over far too quickly.
There are naughty weeds
growing into the manicured grass.
This is the same air I've always secretly smoked into.
This is the same air.

SMOKE

Kingsway

There is a fire underground.
A hazard to humanity.
A hazard to us all.
Invisible, undeniable.
They've dug up the road.
You can see
the rugged insides
of its dark belly.
Dug deep. Mounds of dirt
piled on the tarmac.

How to Lose Your Voice

First, act out the simple things.
Step onto the cold concrete balcony
and scream
until your throat is cracked glass.
Fill up a cup with cubes of ice,
frozen Coca-Cola
and swallow, continuously.
Allow the cold to cut
into your soft pink tissue.
Cough smoke drink shout
in parties in bars
with air clogged and bitter.
Smear with lemon.

Then childish things.
Stop writing. Stop drawing. Stop singing.
Drown out colour, push it
underwater
until it chokes.
Stay blank:
I don't know. Nothing. No idea.
Over time thoughts will turn to dust.

The hard things.
Stay mute.

Stay mute as his voice
crushes down
like a house of tumbling bricks.
Break down your thoughts
scatter them, like seeds,
on his freshly cut grass.
Crush your pen, rip up paper until
you aren't heard
by yourself, by him,
by anyone.

Ask A Village Girl

Ask a village girl: How did she
become a city dweller?
She'll tell you even after four
generations, she never left
the village. That God
brought her here. Twice a day
she roams rows of houses
called galis and nagars,
that were once jungle,
plucking the flowers she
can reach, to make offerings.

Ask a village girl: When did
the highways appear?
She won't give you an exact
date but can say how many
devotees came to her home
to seek her blessings at
Nag Panchmi that year.
How the electricity went
and they used car headlights
to make sure all the mouths
were fed.

Ask a village girl: What does
the young widowed mother
of five look like?
She will show you her sea of
bronze snake statues, point
each one out with her fingers
made of paper bags and
ink, overgrown, stained red
at the tips with daily prayer.
She will look to them to help
heal you when you're sick.

Ask a village girl: Where does
this all end? She will close her eyes
and tell you Padmini comes to
play less and less these days,
that when Padmini disappears
completely, the Gods will come and
take her. You might be stuck
underground on the Bakerloo
line, missing the old moquette,
wishing for slightly more oxygen.

Prey Pray Prey

To be in dialogue with you
turns words
into small burnt offerings
to an ambivalent god

Butter Moon

Your hands, already sticky, are smooshed up against glass.
Breaking silence with the soft mounds of your skin.
Marking time in strawberry smudges.

I remember your mouth making an O
but nothing
and mama's hands welded to the steering wheel.
Her nails gripping the edge of a hard thing.

Outside someone's on their knees.
They're mouthing your name and pointing
to the stars. The trees are dancing up a storm
and the sky is bleeding streetlight.

I can see an orange fist up there.
Where there used to be a moon. It's churning
butter in the air. It's got the whole world in its hands.
Except for you.
It doesn't have you.

You are down here curling
your fingers in on themselves, scraping
back glass.

Our shadows have turned red and gone into hiding.
The car is red.

Your eyes are red.
I pinch your thigh
I imagine it turns blue
and no one says anything.

Mama switches on the headlights.
Mutters a prayer.
I help you with your seatbelt.

Hometown Hypocrisy

I walk down the street.

Its smell, its stink, its debauchery
lies nestled in my bones.

I walk down the street.

It's stunning and dirty all at once
it's twisted in community and antagonism
it is ochre, fuchsia, saffron and gold with clouds dull and grey
it drips with humility yet walks with flamboyance
it's accepting yet intolerable.
You can eat it but you must spit it out.
It spat me out it.
Smoke ganja Girl flash us a smile!
You show me paan rotted teeth.

I walk down the street.

I am your sister
but you're a sister fucker
I am your mother
but you're a mother fucker
wrap up your hair
watch what you wear,
in the bright light of day it's an open palm

in the shadow of night it's a dark, dark fist.

I walk down the street.

Cover up your breasts
cover up your head.
It's religious deliverance
with cat calling.
Open up your legs
but with your palms together

get   on   your   knees.

Open your legs
but close my mouth
drool at my skin
but shame me
unzip your trousers
but zip up my mouth.

It's a wonder,

when we roll up the roads
smoke up the stars
shut off the lights
in the sky,
hide our dirty secrets
in the over-flown bins,

that I feel so comfortably
at home.

When You Tell Me

When you tell me you don't think
I should believe in anything,
I think of my mother kissing
the softest part of my head. Whispering
blessings into my ears.
Placing me in a cot by a prayer mat worn of colour.
The crack of her knees
 as she bends to tell the earth
that she knows where she came from
and to where she will Return.

When you tell me you don't understand,
I wonder if you would have felt differently,
had you known what it was to be born
with angels on your shoulders and prophecies in your palms.
Would you be so quick to free me of my *fictions*.

When you ask me how I can know
I tell you I can't.
But I know I was born of a prayer in my mother's heart
and her mother was born into the dusty echo of the Azan.
You ask me to unravel
what was pressed from cracked lips to upturned palms.
But I can't trace the borders that were broken
or the lines we misplaced.
There is no soil that holds us through time.

There is something buried deeper than our skins.
We spin gold, hang our hopes on the horizon.
Bow our heads to the East and call ourselves home.

You tell me that it's ridiculous.
It's not *rational*.
To leap into infinite space.
To spin your own fictions.

And I imagine the angels on my shoulders spinning plates.

Uber, Uber

We're speeding
in an Uber
through Walworth road,
the driver is in a rush.

I want him to slow down
so I can have your
hands on my legs
your velvet voice
wrapped around me
for just a little longer.

So what are we, I ask
though I'm not
asking for anything, I add quickly
I know, he says
you've been so good
so understanding.

I'm such a dumb bitch
holding onto nothing, I think.

I don't want to put weight on this
that it can't bear, I croak.

Sheena

I have to say everything twice.
You pull my face to your ear,
my voice has disappeared
afraid that you will too
if the words are solid.

Jazz at the North London

Tips on writing, tips on playing
this pen should last this full set.
Roll up, warm up, pen up, pad up,
show me how it works.

Standard improvised, piece
self-penned, segue into Chophouse.
Dark-aired blink, superstar
unhidden, arpeggio unlearned.

Drinks hanging between seats
and fingertips untouched.
He says he wants my body
that he'll take it, should I offer.

It rains outside in Kilburn.

We learn to learn to listen.
We break hungry attention,
we break early affection.
This is blues, after all and I'm a lady.

Green-blooded, canal-smoked
hazy evenings are nostalgia.
He leans past one between us.
He speaks to me through stone.

Roshni

He claims he wants me so bad
the ache makes him
want to pull his teeth out.
I cannot reply through stone.

Still the click-click of the rim
compels him to shove past, place
his plasticine palm on my thigh.
I ask him to only dream of touching.

There's jazz to be heard, mess to be cleared
of unwitting obsession, of misread kindness.
And so here we have another one, drowned in
tears and turned to a city of cynics.

All That Brownness

It's in your blood isn't it.
All that brownness.
The way you roll your r's and make
fans of your hands when you speak.

It gathers in the folds of your skin;
ground spices and plain flour, mango juice and milky chai.
You hold it in your mouth.
Your father's prayers and your mother's worries.
You swallow oceans and the siblings
you will never say goodbye to. They lie
at the bottom of the stack of photos
you keep under your bed, in open coffins
framed by flower garlands, leather skin
fading in black and white.
When you look at their far away faces
you smell rose water.
Feel a wail form in your chest that never escapes.

You wash your feet in the bathroom sink three times.
Put your thumbs in your ears, trace water
round your lobes. You wash off the day and are left
with the distance. Of what lives on in your blood.

After the shop is shut and the children are sleeping,
you drag the the jagged edge of a pencil across

the crisp line of your notebook.
Make to write the letter you start
every night.
To your Ummi Jaan.

Tell her, about the tar covered roads.
The sky that loves nothing more than clouds, the weight
of the coat you wear all summer.
The way rain bounces off the pavement and soaks your silwar
and the people, the people that walk with purpose.
Form lines, sit neatly on trains, tuck into themselves.
Never pushing. Never touching. They wait.
For you to finish before they speak.
They wait to cross roads. They wait always for permission.

Even the dogs here wait to be told before lying down.

But instead of this your thoughts go home
to the saffron sun. To the dust
that dances before it runs its fingers
down the mountain, where the children with the kite
sing songs, count stars, dream of flight.

To the tips of your Ma Jee's fingers touching flames.
Fearless skin burnt gold, turning rotis
on an open fire. To the push and pull of the bazar
There you are
Shoulders brushing, armpits sweating,

cattle herding, fly swatting, ditch dodging azan calling
Everyone talking all at once.
Everything always all at once.

You lie under the shade of a mango tree.
Feel life having touched you all over.
Feel your first born growing inside you,
curse the heat of the sun, cover your face with your duputta.
Look to the sky tinged pink by a thin veil
Count candy floss clouds. Taste sugar on your lips.

The words you make to write fall down in tears.
Draw a route home that tastes of tamarind,
dazzles blood red, emerald green, mehndi orange.

Even without shoes on your feet
you always knew how to dress like a Queen.
To greet the sun in all your colour.

But there are no good words to say, that the home you made
for your children, is not your home. That your mother
died waiting with her prayers, that you father's worry lives on
only in your throat. You hear him when your voice shakes.

And when you have washed away the day
and put the children to bed.
You sit down to write all this.
You sit down to write.

All this.
You sit down to write.

The Lido in Parliament Hill

I enjoyed our Costa del Croydon
afternoon holiday in the sun
in the lido on Parliament Hill,
watching you
watching bodies
and holding you in the water
while you had a wee.
Twice.

You wore a bright blue
Fila bucket hat
that cost you
twenty five quid
from Top Shop
as you wrote work emails
in wet shorts and a John Lennon tee
that screamed,
War is Over
sat with your hands on my legs.

You made me quite wet.

For a while I thought,
he's overwhelmed
by all the women
but then so am I

I guess
he can't think I'm special
but then I saw you
watch my body
as I walked over to you
squeezing water out my hair,
my head bowed
because I felt self conscious
and sat by the pool,
you stroked my crown
and called me beautiful.

We talk shit
and you fall down in the silence
about us
- or you and me.
I hid my face in my hair
like a veil
I cried on your shoulder
and you didn't see;
but we both looked up
when we saw a fight break out
next to the chlorine room
because one man was
looking at a fit girl's knockers
and her boyfriend threatened a fight
all the while his wife and his
superman son

sat wishing it wasn't happening.
Side stepping broad mouthed aggression
the man darts to pool side security
to shout
miiiisssssss!
and had the mouthy girl
and her mouthy man
moved.

You watched her walk past
as she got her food
like she was the meal.

She touched her tits
as they bounced
in her rose pink bikini
her nose in the air
past the man
who ratted them out,
her chest
taunting all the men
not just him
but you as well.

I want more from you
but I have to be
happy
with the way it is too.

My hair dried real fast
on our afternoon
Costa del Croydon holiday
in the lido on Parliament hill.

Watch This Masi

In a Park Royal factory, Minerva Road,
a temporary suspension of the rules
stretches all of a sudden into three decades.
They knock down the old Asda for a new one,
bigger car park, bigger clothes section,
longer hours, endless world food aisles
as if 10-kilo rope-handled bags of basmati
were a novelty, newly available for all.
When the deafening hum of the machines
is finally silenced, when disposable hairnets,
royal blue overcoats and boiler suits,
faded from washing, make a silent exit,
you will pin the lime green name badge to
your polo shirt, learn to sit at the till,
go zero hours, just to have something to do.
You will sit at the tills where your children
sat when they were teenagers, when
they spent their part-time job money
on overpriced clothes from Brent Cross,
secret ciggies and sickly sweet alco-pops.
Your husband's emotional age will be frozen
in time, his tantrums repeating on you like the
overspiced daal you're forced to pick from
the meaty menu of the many local Indian pubs.
Your freedom will remain a spectre as
ghostly as your ability to pass a driving test.

Eventually they'll take you on as an after-hours
cleaner in a council office block in Wembley.
You will take the bus route your retired husband
once drove, while he refuses to drop you off.
The revolution will leave you behind, dear Masi.
Your allies were temporary and bloodthirsty.
The revolution will leave you behind.

Welcome to Abney Park

Waiting for
dawn   God's finger
touches him and he slept
her life was a beautiful memory;
her death a silent grief   bitter
grief   we joke   an angel without
a hand fell asleep   called to rest
sun dappling   not in full shade
but in loving memory   my dear
father   in the service of his count
cherished piece by peace   always
in our thoughts   son   daughter
father   mother   in affliction no
more   Japanese Cherry   (dead-
wood   is   just   as   important)
accidentally killed   because of my
innocence thou hast taken me to
myself   dearly beloved   re-
united   goodbye   god bless

in absence a silent grief

TEMPLES

Except My Mouth is Not a Door

I am a temple, holy water
Idols burning, incense

I rise and rearrange the prayer mats

I press my forehead to your forehead
Put one hand over your eyes and the other
on my heart

I want you to pluck prayers from my palms
Draw rose water from my lips
Plant kisses
in my sacred corners

But you, you grab for my breast
Pull my nipple taught between your teeth
Stretch it far, so far away
I don't know who it belongs to anymore

You part my legs like a snapped jaw
Push your mouth against my mouth
Pin my wrists to the earth and I wonder
Whose sins am I dying for

Except my mouth is not a door, or a window
Or a place to slip your fingers

My mouth is a shrine. Leave
your shoes at the entrance
Wash your feet by the river
I am a temple

Bow your head and bless yourself

An Apology to my First and Only Vibrator

Bzzzzzzzzzzzzzzzzzzzzzzzzzzzzzz
Zzzzzzzzzzzzzzzzzzzzzzzzzzzzzz
The forbidden buzzzzz
of this pink lipstick sized
interloper in my bedroom
yanks me out of childhood.

Ew I have my hands
where I pee,
isn't this hooded thing
where I wee?
I push my lips apart
on both ends of my body.

A waterfall
floods out of me,
my hips start to writhe
this actually feels really nice.

This pink bullet
buzzes right out of my hand,
I start to ride the crest of a wave
and before I know it I've had this thing
they call orgasm
(and I did it to myself!)
I laugh with glee,

flat on my back
my legs spread
I've discovered another use
for my poonani.

The next time,
I sneak it into the bathroom
and after I get nice and clean
I lay down on the bathmat
and get down on it,
legs splayed
I'm starting to get right into this.

....Thing is
after I've had a very nice time,
I forget to take it with me
and there it lays on top of the cistern,
radiating out a call
to my family
and the world!
She's open and good for business!

So while I,
safely ensconced
(for now) in my room
my glow practically nuclear,
my mum
strolls into the bathroom

and zut alors
I've been found out.

Huge with rage
she flings open my bedroom door
my cheeks flushed pink
now turns puce in horror.

She brandishes my lipstick liberator,
oh bollocks
this secret freedom,
it's all fucking over.

Character Study

Question: If I kiss you on the mouth at midnight,
and let you squeeze my tits on a medium-lit side street
in Shoreditch, and then decide that actually I'm tired
and don't fancy much more than that,
am I a bad person?

If I let you into my bed and pass you An Untamed State
to rack up rushed, untidy lines, what will you say when
I simply turn around and tell you I'm not really
up for it and shall we
just go to sleep now?

While you push your manly ways up against me, because boys
will be boys and I think, god, I really can't deal
with this right now, and I say look, I can't, will you think, god
I'm just gonna turn her over
and fuck her anyway?

While I squeeze my brown eyes shut and wish I hadn't got so
stark naked and I will my body to just fall asleep and convince
myself you've got the message, will you wake up in the morning
and think
'fucking weird bitch'?

When I wake up in the morning and offer you tea and toast,
will you reject it for another line and a swig of what's left of
the wine and insist on making me
just give it a little kiss,
just a little one?

Will I be too polite to tell you to please fuck off out of
my house, this is my body, my mum told me it's my temple and
just look at this sacrilege, my body is a temple,
you should be
at my feet worshipping me?

Do I think to myself: this could have been worse,
it definitely could have been worse, but it most certainly
should have been better, what a curse, what a goddamn riddle
are the unwritten rules of free love,
why isn't this shit easier?

From my kitchen window, I watch you walk to the bus stop
in yesterday's clothes. I strip and shower. I scrub the spilt red
wine off my white blinds. I wipe down the remains
of white powder from my nightstand.

I pull my shit together. I carry on with the day.

Let Me Count the Ways

These are the ways you make me feel:
one ice cube clinking in a wine glass on a hot day,
overfilling my mouth with my mum's food
when I haven't been home in a while,
every hair on my head lifting in anticipation,
my first sip of coffee,
confident muscles stretching
before a perfect dive bomb
into a cool, blue pool in front of the lifeguards
and a sign that says no dive bombing.

Family, but the one you choose,
a high note on a violin,
the absolute joy at meeting
a freshly-wrought human being by someone you love,
the split second of the heart leap
when you're swinging on a swing
at the upswing
just before gravity claims you.

Bliss at dancing your hardest to good techno
and you look around
and everyone is beautiful.
The cranium split when you think
a completely new thought
and the world rushes in.

Really thick snow
over everything familiar,
the burn from sitting too close
to a fire.

These are the other ways you make me feel:

a car park in an out of town shopping complex,
when people you don't know ask
'*so, what do you do?*'

Discussing mortgages and London house prices,
sitting in traffic at a time
when you thought you'd beat the traffic,
new builds and words like '*luxury*', '*penthouse*', '*exclusive*',
seeing white girls wear bindis,
really wet feet after a cycle
and being unable to go home and change.

That dread feeling of having to update your phone
and being scared you'll lose everything
and feeling stupid
that you don't know what the cloud is
or how it works
so you put it off until absolutely the last minute
then you end up MANUALLY inputting your numbers
into your new phone
like it's 2003.

Those are the ways you make me feel.

Ghazal – On Woman Adjusting Her Hair
by Degas 1884

I am a chalk and charcoal woman in dust
adjusting my hair in this midnight dust.

Wonder, swathed in waves of broken leaves
I arise from a pond of green dust.

Black bodied, back embodied in black,
back to you, my back to you, I sit in dust.

He scrawls red where my dreams lay
breaking ash orange into dust.

Degas watches me: every bend, every curve,
every jut of my hip, my waist, every line curved in dust.

You want my face turned, blank, broken into dust – You wish –
You watch me forever: nothing, nothing but dust.

The Second Coming

The second coming smells
like the inside pocket
of your father's raincoat.

Lint lined and moth bitten
the second coming has dust in his ears
and a wet sneeze stuck in his throat.

The second coming holds
your hair back.
Slaps you harder than the first.
Hits you
with what feels like the edge of a badly sanded door.

The second coming absolves you,
dissolves you.
Drinks wine from your eyelids,
kisses your stinging tears.
Calls it forgiveness.

The second coming has you
face down.
Palms up.
Legs spread
on a cold floor.
Giving thanks.

Your cheeks are red
with the second coming.
Your lips are hot
from the second coming.
You hold your breath,
for a second.
Coming.

Rosanna

I lean on his freedom. The bleached
blonde of his hair lightens me.
His burgundy, mustard, yellow
painted caravan is my dream, driven.
I sit in its stomach. I cook him houmous,
drink, rock, touch, under absent stars.

Later I will tell you how I dragged
a suitcase heavy as a dead body,
found at sea. Left a week before
my wedding. How white padded walls
surface when I sleep. How I tear holes
into the fabric of my past
(no one can tell) I stitch it up
(no one can see) I drape it over
people I meet, over you, over me.

His eyes stare into the sky when
I touch him. Yet I know, he can
reach for the road in a click,
leave me in white noise
fuzzy uncertain unclear
or he can keep my feet buried
leave me not feeling a thing
leave me feeling everything
with his   one   blank   touch

Sacrifice

The mountain air is pink
and sharp like salt and limes, cut.

Take off your gold earrings
and give them to me, he said
I took them off
he melted them
and together we made a gold calf.

This is the one who saved us, he said
this is the one who led us out into the wilderness.
Worship him.

I breathe the air
and fold down double
at the foot of this false god,
forgetful
it's of my own making,
forgetful
I forged it with my own hand.

The burnished calf glowers.
It saved me
it saved me
it saved so many nameless others
beside me

behind me
before me.

I am on my knees
grateful for any sign
the sign is but my echo
myself at myself.
I am on my knees.

I am on my knees.

Space

Why are you so quiet
Why do you shrink like you don't belong

This space is not big enough to hold you
You and me and them and you, you
Shrink
Shrink like a lotus flower lost
In a dead spring
Lost and you shrink

This space is not for you

They ask
Why are you so quiet
Why have you learnt from others
From unsaid unmoving words that
You should sit quietly wait your turn
Let others take that space

Did no one tell you
Space is infinite

Space is yours for the taking
Space is a void
It is a boundless bountiful beautiful space
Where stars dust and twist and turn

In their space so take your space
Quiet brown girl
It is not white
Despite what they might make you think
In fact, it is black

In this dark matter
Of space
Take it and run
Run or jump or shout or fly
See how far you can take this space
And you will see
That when you close your eyes
The dark space is there
Is mine
Is yours
Is ours

Stand
Shoulders back
Face forward
Eyes fixed like dark planets
Revolving evolving
Involving you
Take this space
It is yours

Own it

Incantation (We are Healing our Sister)

Here is heartbreak, in the heart of our circle.
Walls made of triangles, walls made of light (Triangles of light)
Here is heartbreak, heavy-hearted ache
Waiting to be healed
Sisters, we are healing; we are healing our sister

Hold a mirror up, see ourselves in the heavens
Indiscreet healing, open skies, good heavens
Show her she is heaven, show her she is nature
Show her this is natural (Show her healed)

Triangles of light dance at her feet (At our feet)
Shadows drawn long from her feet (From our feet)
Dancing shadows from our feet begging to be played
Feel our skins blur, draped across thunderclaps
Clap, clap, thunderclaps, smack, smack, boom bap,
Gusts brought forth from our thunderclaps
We know each other, we are each other
We know one another (We are one)

See how we are healing
See her heart opening
Pleasure starts in our hearts
We start in the heart
(We open our hearts)

Here is her heart Here is pleasure
Here is healing She is healing
She is we We are she We are one
We are heaven
We are healing, sister We are healing.

Sunnah Khan, Sharan Hunjan,
Roshni Goyate and Sheena Patel are
4 BROWN GIRLS WHO WRITE.

In the summer of 2017 a group of friends, some of whom were strangers to one another, got together on a boat on the Thames to share their poetry and drink prosecco. Amongst these friends were Sunnah, Sharan, Roshni and Sheena. The four resonated deeply and found strength in each other's voices.
They created a space to nurture each other's writing and share in vulnerability. A year later, with many new poems written, shared and performed as a collective, here they are:

4 BROWN GIRLS WHO WRITE.

This is their first collection.

Special Shoutouts to:

Alia @A8LIA   Bilan @BILANSU
Arti   Bhav   Jaya
Aish   Raïf
Shivanee
JD

IG: @4BROWNGIRLSWHOWRITE

4 BROWN GIRLS WHO WRITE

Designed by – BK Imisson
                bkimisson@gmail.com

Published by – FEM Press
                georgia@femzinelondon.com

                www.femzinelondon.com

Cover art by – Sheena Patel